Pilgrim's Flower

RACHAEL BOAST was born in Suffolk in 1975. *Sidereal* was published in 2011 and won the Forward Prize for Best First Collection, and the Seamus Heaney Centre for Poetry Prize for Best First Collection. She lives in Bristol.

Rachael Boast

Pilgrim's Flower

PICADOR

821.92
BOA

First published 2013 by Picador
an imprint of Pan Macmillan, a division of Macmillan Publishers Limited
Pan Macmillan, 20 New Wharf Road, London N1 9RR
Basingstoke and Oxford
Associated companies throughout the world
www.panmacmillan.com

ISBN 978-1-4472-4217-8

9 8 7 6 5 4 3 2 1

A CIP catalogue record for this book is available from the British Library.

Printed and bound by CPI Group (UK) Ltd, Croydon, CR0 4YY

Visit www.picador.com to read more about all our books
and to buy them. You will also find features, author interviews and
news of any author events, and you can sign up for e-newsletters
so that you're always first to hear about our new releases.

Contents

La première enterprise fut, dans le sentier déjà empli de frais et blêmes éclats, une fleur qui me dit son nom.

Pilgrim's Flower

I

The Place of Five Secrets

Resembling Cocteau, the two statues in the pillars
of the fireplace have been busy inside the scenery,
guarding the room where Belle takes her meals

bemused by every fine detail, every gilded hand-held
object offered her, their faces turning as she takes
a moment to look around, lost in the five secrets

of Bête who is not himself, even on a good day.
Suffering the blind world and its lack of faith,
for her he makes sure all the doors will open

by themselves, all the rooms light up
to lead her through the dark that cannot lift
until her love's second sight revives him as he is,

and not as others see him; *ne faut pas regarder
dans mes yeux* turned around by key, mirror,
horse, glove, and the rose at the centre of it all.

Re-reading Akhmatova

And so I, stepping somnambulistically,
entered the life and the life frightened me
   —Northern Elegies

I'm not sleepwalking, although the border
between sleep and waking
isn't all that clear . . . I've heard the echo
of you pacing up and down:

you left the house, only to stamp out
the cold in the bread queue; you left
the black earth, its buried hoard,
but now I've drawn up your necklace of words,

a blue rosary that tells me the border
between the here and hereafter
isn't all that clear . . . For I've long owed

these sparks to your trail, unable
to keep up when, behind my ribs,
the living word remains inarticulate.

Caritas

(St Andrews Cathedral)

These stones speak a level language
murmured word by word,
a speech pocked and porous with loss,
and the slow hungers of weathering.

And there, in the broken choir, children
are all raised voice, loving the play of outline
and absence where the dissembled god
has shared his shape and homed us.

At the end of the nave, the east front stands
both altered and unchanged,
its arch like a glottal stop.

And what comes across, half-said
into all that space, is that it's enough
to love the air we move through.

Other Roads

IV. Dun Holm

Across the causeway of Lindisfarne
to the high ground,
St Cuthbert's coffin-bearers
came to a miraculous halt.

Only prayer could get them
on the road again, to a place looped
by time's immaculate river.
Above it, the cathedral is a bird of prey

guarding her nest of relics,
eyes in the front and the back
of her head; a teacher,
or prophetess, alert

to the flooded fields of Lothian
and Borders, to how each county
resists the next, Lords of province
glaring from the buried dark.

V. Compass Plant

One sprig should do, in a wayfarer's satchel,
to allow for the loss of all bearings
until you're standing
where the road stops you,

as a road should never do,
closed off even as it continues
towards the hollow hill of Eildon
in a long grey disguise.

Think about it, you're diverted,
as if you'd seen into the earth,
drawn like a magnet
through a field of old stories

where borders are buried
to a Rhymer's Stone –
take it as a blessing,
with no thought for the road.

Reciprocity

Now you no longer drink so much coffee
you tell me you've nothing to say –
until, when I ask for your umbrella
having made my visit, as always,
impromptu like summer rain,
you answer with a yarn – *and then
there was St. Martin, tearing his capella in half.* . .

If *happiness is tedious*, how is it you're stimulated
only when I'm about to leave –
and so delay me, flagging up
that it's thresholds we love,
that tear us apart; our eyes looking
back and forth for the little chapel
we've entered in, that place we cannot stay. . .

Double Life

(Thomas Chatterton)

In the pounding of ochre and crumpling of parchment
you'd guard the work of antiquating your life,
illuminated by your own de-centering
behind a casement of stained glass.
You were bored of the mercantile and paid no heed to it
and when someone asked your name
coughed politely and walked the other way.

Always in sight of Our Lady on the Red Cliff,
this church made you old before your time,
has imitated time, as it has imitated you,
your fate sealed into you like a nave
scrolling over a series of memorial stones
to a place-on-high; guises revealed not as forgeries
but the mutable self fluttering by candlelight.

Fire Door

And isn't a song, or a poem . . . a game language
plays to restructure time?
  —Brodsky

Straight down the line the day after
the night before, I found myself looking
back to small fires burning
at the edge of upturned fields,
to the *nack bar* abandoned in a yard

after Ladybank, the sun bearing down
on the lay of the land,
the Lomond hills like a woman
sprawled across a borderline
taking in the reach of the long sky;

past Markinch and a place called Star,
past Burntisland by the flaring sea,
and into Haymarket to change
and change again, wondering
if you'd made the same connection as me:

how we'd been in the right place
at the right time – you knocking loudly
from the other side of the fire door,
and me burning my hand as I pushed
the metal bar to get you back indoors

saying *we've been through this one before* –
so much so, these sleepers crossing over
the rivers of other lives lead again
to the descending sun flaring above a line
of cloud as I return to the place

from which I started out, a place that could
trick me into thinking no time at all
had passed, were it not that I remembered
your flash remark: *it's alright, it's the door
that's on fire,* you said, *not the spaces on either side.*

Homage

On each visit the waves would follow me down
the narrow street in sentences breaking out
of language to tell me *homage* means going
back to the same place until it knows you –

and I'd hesitate, listening for the way we came
out of the sea with our hands in a vow of give
and take to its turning page which reads
the narrow street leads to a double key.

Cocteau Twins

I've heard the phrase *between you*
and me too many times to believe

it to be true, but between me and you
there was Cocteau, wagging his testimonial

finger, as usual, while flat out on the floor
with my arms in receipt of the flower

of thought, palms upwards, I envisaged
the inside eyes of his hands remaking words

for a song that is a drawing that is a film –
that is, a poem; and in the middle of all this

the books on the shelves float down while
falling upwards, slipping out of their jackets

as the naked petals of their pages turn
into mirrors, which is to say, they blossom.

By Appointment Only

(Charles Wesley House)

for Thom

Along the corridor of keyboards, footstools,
reverb units and amplifiers to the backyard
where, up the steps and into the neighbour's garden,
you remember where you are: two houses

nestled between office blocks, halls of residence,
dull facades reaching up through
the minimalist sky they give rise to.
And at the end of the path, past fig and pear,

between glorious borders of mint and lavender,
honeysuckle and peace-flower,
a sundial etched with timelines

like the lines in the palm of the hand
records a music obedient
to the spheres of the heralding angels.

Losing My Page

Nothing was ever straightforward with you
and so, instead of returning to where
I left off, I re-entered the poem
from afar — it hardly mattered where —

and eventually reached the same clearing
marked, I'd noticed, by the hands of time
held up in prayer, where I'd seen you before —
or thought I had — at the midnight hour

you rhyme yourself with. Page after page
the light would change, to dark and back again,
reminding me of someone who, when put

on the spot, knows the dance of gain and loss
by the secret fidelity of moving
from one foot to the other, to the other.

To St Mary Redcliffe

They hid this Art that no Man finde it cann.
— Thomas Norton

I

That said, the waves, punctual, lucid,
quick-tongued, tug at the hulks of the boats
while out on the balcony
of the Watershed café
there's a man who's not the same man

he was when walking the street:
here he gains in presence, a Harlequin
distinguished above the silt-line
of coffee cups. St. Mary's delivers up
her bell-canticle as he rummages

for his plundered diamond necklace
in the high wind that carries
a wave of light diagonally
from quayside to quayside
as if life were a matter of practice.

II

Falls and uprisings ghost the old city
in its annals and peripli.
Stopping on my walk I glare across
the water at the banks and new-builds
on one side, and on the other,

the drinking holes of Bordeaux Quay,
taking note of how that old Pantalone,
Plutocracy, has established his kingdom
at this celebrated crossroads
and thought to get away with it.

I walk on. The sun's afloat,
jubilant as a smashed champagne glass
left over from a wedding party,
while everything has that look
of looking so near and so far.

III

Behind these merchant streets
a pair of mute swans, feathers spread
like fish-bones or a full-blown rose,
position themselves in the sun's glare,
knowing, with fierce clarity,

how to become unseen
in their watery chamber, with its erratic
chandelier, its bright invisibility
(bright enough to exclude me)
until she's submerged beneath him,

not far from where Norton supposedly
got up to no good with his thieving mistress.
Better not to give a damn, say nothing,
then rise up dripping with light
surfacing, in a moment, heaven knows where.

IV

Knowledge of the library's back catalogue
returns me to the Harlequin by the river
who, let's say, reappears on College Green,
in the upstairs reference room,
erasing the tale of two regal lovers –

only, he does it in reverse,
so taken in that he has to draw a line
somewhere and so draws it thus:
He lays down his arms
while she relaxes the letter of his law,

for the burden was heavy, but the back
is now broad, broad enough for her
to roll him over and write a new decree:
you are my city, my body politic,
and I, your Lazuli Lady of [. . .]

V

The Chaotic Pendulum is tucked away
in the north transept. It's not far,
but the route gets complex,
and I'm diverted around toxic investments
and half-built car parks, sneaking glances

at the boats in their moorings –
Salamander, *Sappho*, *Sidereal*, lined up
like notes in a glockenspiel –
before turning into Three Queens Lane
and Canynge Street. It's mid-afternoon

by the time I cross the road and arrive
at St Mary Redcliffe. I walk down the aisle,
in the footsteps of Coleridge,
seeing him in a swan-skin waistcoat
about to lose his cause.

VI

Is this tubular arm not moving
from a cross with a weight nailed to it
by which the Lords of Time and Chaos
demonstrate – through the agency
of water – that the Age of Wonder

is very much with us?
And isn't this a miracle of rare device,
a timepiece at odds with time,
but on which, nevertheless,
we can rely to wake us from inertia?

And even though this church was rebuilt,
it's said, from the stolen lapis
of a devoted Pierrot, she's steadfast,
spirited of solid stone tested in the fire.
She's been worked into love-speech, has she not.

VII

In this brief pantomime the only black
and white (besides the floor tiles
of Mary Redcliffe) is this unscripted
bolt from the sky without which
the big sway of watery curtains

would have been drawn over the scene
long ago. Lost and found, forgetting
the time, my route takes me home
into the heart of this green-shouldered
gold and silver city, this bell-lovely city,

with Norton on my arm, his morale intact
like a glass-hulled boat steering
between mud-flats that glisten and flag
the stark estuary of the Severn
as it is in the haven of the mind.

The Withdrawing Room

(7 Great George Street)

The seventh of ten bells on sprung-coils
outside the basement kitchen is rung
by a man in the upstairs drawing room.
Such is this house of servitude. So too,
the call sounded sometime before
for a young Devonian to drop in
one September afternoon in 1795.
Take this as *a repetition in the finite mind*
and in the sweetest way possible
he never actually materialized,
such are the echoes of this house of sugar.

But suppose that one man is reading aloud,
pacing the boards, up and down,
while another stares at the view
of the Cathedral's medieval tower
where, later, a marble bust of his own head
stands in a stellate alcove.
Which leaves a third man who,
absenting himself from the game
at play, is all the more animated
for having noticed a painting of the Avon Gorge
to which his back is now turned.

He's just seen how all things are cut
from the same rock, all things
a repeating echo of the mind of God.
Has seen, in the water,
an image of recollection, so much so
that everything looks inside out
and the ornate room – the bone china,
the house of cards on the soft tabletop –
will return one day to its prima materia
while we'd remember reality the more
by mirroring the long attention of the river.

The Notebook

(Coleridge's tour of Scotland)

The jaunting-car was too fast for your eye —
you'd rather have got out and walked,
staying true to your allegiance
to local epiphany until nature knew
her secrets would be safe with you.

A field of potatoes in flower, the intense
eye of the poppy took time, testified
that a mind which thrives
on the universal truth of detail
is not the mind of a tourist.

And so you parted company,
staring out the black mountain brays
of Glen Coe before going the distance —
two hundred and sixty-three miles
along the song-line of your withdrawal.

By night, your head a north-pointing
compass, the pathways in your brain
insisted on a human pace,
a notebook damp with memory,
with brandy, with rain.

Deer Park

For a path is an un-going, congruent with the steep gradient,
a scar impressed across the landscape, prepared ground.

Turning this way and that, it is a parting, as if a stag
was buried deep in the hillside of the dream of itself.

We need more wild creatures in our landscapes –
at least I think that's what you said, you spoke so softly.

You spoke as a priest might speak – *what I do not have*
makes room for you; these feet are your feet; I have no roost,

no offspring. I am roughshod, an odd man in black
poking the chervil – and as I looked over at you

your eyes were steeped in distance, carrying the dark
in the openness of your heart, master of camouflage.

St Fillan's Gallery

Back on the coastal path again and up along Cove Wynd,
past the place where St Fillan stayed up all night
working by his luminous left arm,

reminding me not to wander off the track
which, for old times' sake, I retrace, stopping
for a miraculous plate of bread and fresh herring

and the usual crowd: puffins and a collage of shovellers,
the over-colourful gulls, and right behind me
a preening heron – though nothing like the one

I saw by Shore Head, dishevelled in a rockpool
while the sea slammed in – and even as I'd give
all this back to you, it's gone:

the grey light in which the oystercatchers,
coming quickly at me, are tuned
to each incoming wave without having to look.

Rosary

(Fontannyy Dom, 1926)

The third marriage on the horizon,
a clean sheet with an art critic, wasn't to be
and with one boiled egg between
the three of them, they carried on
for what must have seemed like a century.

Already outliving her contemporaries,
imagine the weight of it –
checking the hands of women for rings,
not because you want them,
but because of the density of the heart's intrigue

demanding to know what it's like
to have such a star orbit your finger.
She gets up to leave
before the glint can reach her
and she'll grow tired of prayer, so very slowly.

Bolshoy Fontan

Turning the other cheek so you wouldn't see
the shore I was staring towards,
the salt stains on my litmus face,
you could have been anybody –
were it not that I can tell your eyes a mile away,
innovating what they can of me
without losing the sense that the beauty
they perceive is as much me as you.

And what distances we covered –
the holiday we couldn't have
going just according to plan,
all the signs pointing back along a path
we hadn't walked on, love unmaking itself
at the bathetic edge of a Black Sea.

Balmerino Abbey

I gave a small fee, as the notice asked me,
thinking it worth my while to slink among stones,
walk across walls, try the weathered steps leading
to an absent place –

and almost started back; but a wooden cross
hammered into the ground, marking the altar,
led me on beyond to a Spanish oak, or,
observed from the left,

a heavy-breasted woman in whose figure
nested something almost mammal and merging
with her flecked bark, on the verge of flinching out
of a long half-sleep.

I could then have started back; but, noticing
where the south wall was, knelt into the snowdrops
to hear those delicate downward trinities
spread their small rumours

until near in the air, I saw un-cloistered,
bright with the memory of homage and songs,
the face of the northern breeze, lyre of Aurai.
Then I was ready

but then, over to the west, saw how starlings
on their murmuring flight path had come to rest,
dropping into line on the roof of a barn
one by one by one

before lifting off again and inclining
into that vanishing point of airborne forms
un-blackening at the narrowest angle
of themselves [. . .]

After Sappho

On this dark earth
the night ambush at the blockades,
peace envoys in the arms trade,
operation Odyssey, the shock and the awe –
all these are an insult to the power of love.

Understand this, it's easy:
a thousand ships in pursuit of a woman –
who only wanted to hide her face
in one man's embrace –
stood no chance against the undertow

of love's will . . . Which brings me back to you.
How I too, overcoming the checkpoints
of the mind, slipped past the guards
with their yes or no answers, outwitted Mars
and went after you.

I carry in my heart this clannish chant
for a compass. And always
it knows where you are
just as you know, by the light of the stars,
that our love's a moon too new to be seen.

The Window

To those walking the river path
this morning, I have the luck of the view
while remaining invisible,
undressed behind the mood of the weather.

That would cheer you up. I can see you
looking over, waving perhaps,
trying to make out my long arms,
my long legs, the long shadow of my smile –

for you've been on both sides of this window,
seen how people stare at nothing in particular,
nothing they could put a name to;
seen how water lends itself to white cloud –

to anything that's transitory – as though it's easier
to love the things that don't stay.
I'll look for your looking one day, before I
become window, become view, become rain.

Moonlight

(After Cocteau)

Each half of the heart deep in geography
displays the relief of its departments.
The moon captured by the sun's photography
is the subject of my astonishment.
Endymion your lover or not your lover?
As the absurd pin is mad for the magnet's allure,
as the gun makes afraid the sanctuary,
as the beauty in the wood dreams aloud,
I count to three before sleeping: *Une,*
deux, trois. Endymion disrobes the moon.

Song of

We are such stuff as dreams and prayers are made of,
hardly here, a masterpiece of wings reading

the parallel script of the sky in black and white,
the flower which blossomed twice, four-petalled

then five, came back to life, like a prolonged dream,
your eyes on mine and my eyes on yours,

like the calm inside the storm. Do you recall
following in the dark by ear, hearing the dream

of the prayer leading the both of us past
floating walkways between the walls

of a labyrinth of a hundred shut windows
to the transiting rose where the scent remains

scene by scene – there, the blue and green of the posh
peacock, lush sofas – here, pomegranate reds. . .

II

Songs

(After Machado)

If you hold it up to the light it's clear
there's little love in a diamond;
better the bright coal whose heat
forces it apart into a hundred fires —
for, like love, poetry is the raw form
of things tended in the grate
of the heart: no one has ever
blown on a diamond and found fire,
but the poet entices light from dark
by the pressure of thought and its spark —
with no desire to remove impurities
and make an anonymous, pristine thing.
And because your name will never be found there
I can't write beneath a cold, oblivious sky. . .

Anon

for Thomas and Charlotte

I

Wræclast: The Way of the Stranger, *Outlaw's Lane*,
Exile's Track. For old times' sake, I walk its furlong
of white nettle and sorrel,
a grassy mohican running up the middle,
to drink my morning coffee
in the sticks – suspecting
it's sugared with riddles, which it is.

II

A whispering grows wild
along the lanes and in the meadows,
says *listen out for a hare's breath, a hawk's beard,
the pierced ear of a fox, for words will not serve you
under these skies*, but I can say this:
everything looks as if it could be peeled away
like paper, not just once, but twice, and again.

III

Careseia: Isle of Cress, as they'd have said it was,
the dead entrusted there, encircling the church,
their bones laid like cutlery in the peppered ground.
Then down the hill and across the cart-wash
to the house with the horse's tail hanging from the eaves.
Light leans in, the colour of parchment,
opens the rooms like entries in a diary.

IV

A rooftop settlement, green moss basks in its conquests
and private concerns; staid by homeliness,
witness to generations of moody billows.
Leaded windows tilt in the wall
each with a latch like a wrought-iron arachnid.
The yard always gets wind of my return –
a listening post, the eaves creep forwards.

V

At some late hour I'd unlock the side-door,
pressing its enamel tongue for the cool shush
outwards onto flagstone, then walk in the direction
of Broad Riddle to see for myself Lesser Riddle
and Further Riddle after their bounty,
years having passed, and the family line
long harvested, a crop of namesakes.

VI

I set out one day to look for the Chapel of the Rood
of Good Rest, owned by locals you never saw.
The nettles in the doorway like cautions
grew above my head, so I ploughed through them
to sit in the pew of my shortcomings
counting and recounting my blessings
of which there was always one missing.

VII

Unmade of laid stone and raised walls, I notice now
what I thought was missing in the tall Oak
and the circling blossoms of the rag trees,
the lintels of their roots stranded
in the open ground: for see no road comes near,
and a rush of young ears stalked firm
in the cornfield reads like scripture.

VIII

And here's another school, under my feet. Not a ruin
or a page from history but the old, near earth,
the world as mirror for what's unseen.
We can't see by walking up and down
what we've sown, what we've dropped
into the furrows of our years
and covered over: the world's this mirror.

IX

Walking the tributaries that weave between
the old wool villages, their wash-stones,
well-heads and babble ongoing, I gain the lift
of the huge sky where time is a camouflage
for the unchanging. To one side, the last lit house,
to the other, spark and fettle catching across
the quilt of harebell, hawksbeard, foxglove.

X

This urge for the uncivil, for farm track
and furrow, comes from knowing
words will scatter like crows
in a moment's tarry.
It's as well to stay here on a level
with the sun's descent, and say:
let me be unlooked for, let no one call my name.

St Mary's Quad

for Ciaran Carson

As it happens, this inscription carved around
the silent fountain, all but coming away
from the freckled stone, retains enough

of the strength of its origin for your voice
to bring it back to life, seeing as I ask
what it means, for *this* is what I mean:

to remedy the broken tune falling flat
inside its trefoil, and in so doing
set it in motion as we wait here

with our hands rapt behind our ears
in the harmony of equal measure,
on the first day of the year's zodiac.

Miracles

(After Cocteau)

Blessed Virgin, is it true, in your health spa
that you appear to the blind and the shut-eyed?
Breton sailors see you in their yards –
I take them at their word – that you are attired
like a swallow, in the colours of a brief visitor,
on a background of forget-me-nots, on lace-paper:
that the cry of the gull resembles your cry
each time you evaporate, leaving their names inscribed.

Annunciation in an Elevator

Always when you're ready it happens – like it
or not: the elevator was going up, the vision

still not dawning, as if it had been something
ordinary, a reverse gravity held in place

by ropes of steel. Forgetting all about this
overlay of worlds, with you already its darling,

you were discussing miracles in the third person
with Picasso, wiping your plate unawares

with bread, wondering how it is we don't melt
in the bath tub. Then, down the back lane

and to bed, or not to bed – either way, the threshold
of the remembered angel lasted for days,

refusing, as they will, to remain unspoken for,
taking shape only through the written word.

The Scribe's Migraine

(Ruth 3)

And so it was that morning fell open
into the shape lips might make
after a song of high praise,
or like water pouring from a jug.
But then it sets in again:
last night's lines, still illumined,
burning in the shut book of his brain,
resume their discordant tones.

Midday, and the doors he calls at close.
No share of meat with a sprig
of rosemary, no shadows
in the street, not one raised voice.
The trees shoulder the darkness
as he follows the violet paths
to where the wind moans ad nauseam
and his vision's cut with rain.

And he'll try again under candlelight,
night's rainbow, with an unknowing
closer to home than home itself
yet exiled from the home
he could have chosen. And so
it came to pass at midnight
that the man was afraid,
and turned himself: and, behold

The North Porch

(Thomas Chatterton)

Not knowing until the moment comes
at some late hour, who you are,
or might be; raving in the Lunacy

of Ink, the night tapering, dissimilated
from papyrus, from scraps, from daily bread;
the three-fold bosses of tail chasing tail

after tail; looking out at the gospel
in capitals, level with the buttresses,
led back, time and again, to the image,

not of the builder but of his masonry;
of dream-vision, miraculous city,
the marvellous breasts of the girls in the doorway. . .

The Charity of Thomas Rowley

Forget Dr Johnson who got his backside
stuck up the winding stair of Mary Redcliffe,
playing critic to one he considered
an un-tutored *provincial* pauper,

for having imagined that double-whammy
negotiating the staircase to your garret of ice
and thunder, it came as no surprise
the room where you'd write was electric,

copying from books on Heraldry, Antiquity,
on Music, Metaphysics, Astronomy,
Mathematics – the flash of your pale blue eye

disturbing the dust, over-bright, incalculable –
saved clean from the storm by an alter-ego
who gave you his semecope, his silver, his smile.

St Anne-in-the-woods

All that's left are the street names
Chapel Way, Pilgrims Wharf, Angels Ground –
but all the same I follow the clues
down into the valley, knowing my way
by innocent folly, until I find St Anne's Well,
a sorry sight, a stopped miracle.

Once sister to Walsingham and Canterbury,
Matriarch of earth and water, port and harbour,
I inspect the curious offerings,
pulling aside lumps of concrete
until I'm a well-wisher in reverse –
a fool that rushes in as sometimes we must.

Three Poems After Rioja

I

Lap Dissolve

Eels of the evening size up the rug,
extend from oil-filled radiator
and recharging laptop,
its one square eye dissolving
into ropes of light caught on camera
as we accelerated across the Tay Bridge.

II

That's the one you took, moments after
we delayed the traffic by discussing
tolls with the man inside the box,
found we'd created a whiplash of lights
that followed us out of the city
turning chthonic as we hit the back road.

III

Close Shave

There is no narrow escape from desire –
just step on it, while I ask this:
if the food of love were eels,
would you deny these fingers
as they slip across your face,
feeling for each brittle starting point?

The Conference

Footfall along the shadowed aisle
of the college chapel
foretold you arriving epiphanic
in my face; the booming voice –
a decibel above ego, forgetting to switch

off your lapel microphone –
was spot on: "It's page one hundred
and thirty four." The high heaven's
vaulted halls echoed you; the cold walls
of the chapel porous to your voice

and its harmonic precision,
while members of the delegation
ferocious for the toffee of knowledge
harassed me in the interval FFI
to which I replied, *FOFY*.

The Flowers

*For in a house that serves the Muses
there must be no lamentation: such a thing
does not befit it.*
  —Sappho, *Fragment 150*

What planted this smile on my face
is the comedy of how a man will embrace
two loves. When I caught sight
of the one spray red and the other white
and knew neither were intended for me,
I might have assumed I had mistakenly
retraced my steps to say goodbye
a second time for the convenience of a lie –

for realizing he'd thought to buy them
part way through our conversation
lent me a line as though straight from Machado,
and never was it said with more bravado
that there's nothing to lament
when *she has the rose while I smell the scent.*

Milestones

What can Sappho's Leap have been beyond this?
  —S. T. Coleridge

They had the map while you out-walked them,
so much so that at every inn they chanced on
you'd already spent the night,
drunk the wine and polished off
the oatcakes reserved for *strays*.

The misunderstandings were such
that after an evening of nervous laughter
at Loch Katrine, you were advised
to make your own way home. Soon as.
So instead, you went north

along the Great Glen Road,
regaining your liberty in burnt shoes;
across Wade's High Bridge
with the void in your stomach enlarged
by the long scope down to the Spean

where, slipshod and open to suggestion,
the journey falls into place:
on to the Moray Firth, your only map
the highs and lows of the landscape
opening in front of your eyes.

Herm

Of course I found omens in the far trees
the wind had shaped into gods and ravens
and then one day I caught up with them,
adding to their deliberate detail
my own brief shadow.

What You Will

(or, Twelfth Night)

I kept my wineglass empty at mealtimes
so I might remember you in that transparency

then stole away from the house of festivity
for the silver decorations the sun creates

in the tops of the trees. I didn't think.
I became a breeze, as though a piece of heaven

had landed in me so I'd suddenly know my way:
circling the church by the floating harbour

I re-read that look in your eye, recalling
the blue boy on bread and water and the rhymes

of the hour, the moon conjoining Jupiter
among the seven hundred poems of the sky.

Aubade

In the emollient night of roses and paraffin,
of burning hands and of all that burns

of broken sleep piecing together what for
so long had remained lost of what was lost

not in the dark but in the fire of the dark
in the night and in the oil of the night

of everything you were led to believe in,
everything stays secret until – one morning –

you put your hands through the touch
of the unfinished light and took it back.

Strength of Song

Here they come, the duet possessed,
you might say, by the charm

of their own silence; two lamps
in the nether-light moving against

the tide, moving in little fucks of the water
through the all-in-one, seeming

to have noticed what they're up against,
confronted by the other-wise pull

yet settling for it nevertheless, into its dots
and dashes, into the unison of incessant script

as they repeat the upward lift of their necks
in that language with which they say

bread for a song or song for our bread —
whatever. I'm Porgy, she's Bess.

Tearing and Mending

(the first three minutes and seven seconds of
'Hiroshima Mon Amour')

After rewind and replay it's still unclear
how the burned skin of the embrace

flinches into intimacy, into focus,
then changes into dust, then rain;

the tenderness of love's erotesis,
the way her fingers press into the soft

of his back, into its folds and the otherness
of its give asking questions she can never

forget. He answers back, his body ablaze
with remembered dawns, each movement

of his mouth cracked with the fricative
of war; their torn hearts hiding the memory

of shadow and stone, transfigured
into rain, then dust, then flesh and bone.

Redressing Marsyas

For you I bring all the woodwinds
back out of the trees
to give music to your words,

the flutes and the reed pipes
buried under the pines
at a time when your expectations

were lower than anything on earth;
when the stories of this upside down world
would hide their true meaning

under the skin of the imagined,
the rind of fable,
no thanks to Ovid's tall tales –

for even Alcibiades, drunk out of his skull
in the lap of Socrates,
could see through the outward form

and find gods inside a hollow man;
and yet a sober man, for all his spin,
sees only what he wants to see:

air in a raw lung, or the twin arteries
of hubris and overstepping,
and whatever else suits his perversion.

The image alone of Marsyas,
metamorphosed
into the clearest river in Phrygia

by the grief-silver of his mourners
leaves me paying my respects
to what's always left unspoken;

that you deserve more than a gift
that didn't open, lost libretto
for a satyr who, in another life,

we see balancing a wine glass
on his upright phallus, his skin
unmarked, his hair and beard lush

as the tussocks of Olympus;
songs you tore to pieces
thinking the stakes were too high,

as if the music of chance
and the palace it led to
were meant for someone other than you.

Spring Tide

Tonight from the window the river's back-flow
borrows from an obscured moon,

new born, making the hours
become moments more than themselves

which perhaps is what time is for.
You've just left this edgeland

of everything that's out of our hands
even as it belongs to us; which is why

my face is as bright as water
thinking back to you for the sake of it

inwardly lit with a love of the weather
you bring here; this long calm like a path

we're guided down by the call
of an owl. Always so, it's always so.

The Garden Path

for the man who is beautiful is beautiful to see
and yet the good man will at once beautiful be

Dedication

You led me this way, past the sound
the otter makes, crouched by the water's edge
for water's cold clear wakefulness

and into a stretch of time
for old times' sake, a long-since,
a small hour that doesn't fit anywhere,

a camouflage of concentration
in which everything gains
the slow stealth of the same selfhood.

I

Within the hour, the lift and fall
of the river will disorder
all my senses, so much so
I close my eyes at night, my body

confluent with the supple tide;
have slept deep in that feeling
dreaming of your arms like water
as the river and the riverbank

soak in to each other; have seen
mirrors in my sleep – something
pressed so close you can't tell
who's above and who's below.

II

I keep a low profile at a level
with loosestrife and the roots
of the willows, learning the ropes

of how to look at water
as the colour of nothing
and so have nothing to lose,

letting it body me, hollowed out
like a long-eared owl listening
to the sleep of flowers

within which the rivers in the sky
say that on Venus, a day
is almost as long as a year.

III

It's a low ebb for paw prints
in the silt of the bank,
otter or mink; but either way, feminine,
just as a slipknot will steady

but come easily undone.
The river knows how to keep going –
what it loves already belongs to it:
a double oxbow, autumn in her red leaves

coming loose from summer,
the splayed repose of the willow.
I waited seven years this week
to have you here.

IV

The river's in spate; what remains of the day
is reflected there in red and gold
as dark on dark
doubles its searchlight stars.

I look hard for you, for what's left
when you've gone –
spilt water steadied into beads
by the side of the bed, the sheets pouring down.

V

Life's precarious, a bed of water;
the sleep that comes
comes like an untying of ropes
that burn until I let the last one go,
the last small fire my hand can hold.

VI *On Sappho*

Inside the cabin of the boat both worlds
come together in the diminuendo
of its name, so that last night's *Bateau Ivre*

today becomes the steady sounding-hut
for the rain, and my ears the ballast
for an Orphic hymn, which is how come

those long-armed men I love sail straight
past me with their blond goddesses,
thinking I'll still be here when they return

with the tide but how am I to know. I've eyes
only for this silver portal, while *Sappho*,
hollow instrument I'm holed up inside

makes sensitive my line of sight,
water-levelled by diplomacy; of the river,
of the wine, of the inevitable lyric of time.

VII

Once upon a time you proposed
on the banks of the Lethe
proposed that when we'd crossed over
we'd forget Eros and Agape

VIII

With too much time on my hands
I practise the lover's knot
and get it wrong, over and over –
I'm like this with everything,
with skin like rope-burn,
a taut length, a 'crossing turn'.

IX Paean

The river's a mystery school.
I half expect to see a singing head
floating past the prow to break
the wave of my known world.
The swan, to whom water
is something that can be
written on, spreads her small
rumours until the river
is a chorus, a portal into which
I take a long leg-length
step down from the wet bank
just to hear the echoes sing true.

X

Dropping my favourite pen in the water,
I reach for the boat hook
to plough the riverbed,
face down over the edge of the bow
where an underwater furrow
plumes into a milky way,
an oracle, a fragment
no less lovely for what it lacks.

XI

The river goes back
a long way,
its turn of phrase
as archaic as when
Sappho first described
the moon as silver,
and love sweet-bitter.

So if words fail to surface
I'll give up the search,
hum the old tunes –
Moon River, *Deep River* –
with strings plucked
not strummed, modesty
the rule of thumb.

XII

It need hardly be said how precarious
it all was, which is precisely why it's lasted,
blessed by water, light's emissary, wind-anchor.

XIII

A pen glides on its own white image
knowing nothing of it, serving nothing
but the water-music strung from the future
in the shape of a lyre: feathers folded
it watches the water, that true emblem
like a transparent sheet spread between
two realms, alive to everything.

XIV

The full moon river is flowing as fast as paper,
dog-eared waves and creases intercepting
each another like memories of past and future.
Turn the double key the other way — I'm silhouetted
on the balcony, surprised by swans asleep
on the long mirror, Jupiter's searching light
sweeping the path you made for me.

The Hands of Jean-Maurice

(After Rimbaud)

Jean-Maurice has slender hands,
hands that protrude with the song-bones of birds
and know the world by fluttering in tandem.

Did they brush against an empyrean woman,
these hands of love, to resemble a flash of lightning?
Have they tossed roses at the burning feet of Marias?

Hands which, smelling of marigolds, move
through mirrors? What handsome dream held them
in animation of itself, the shape of precise miracles?

The back of these hands, tanned with the almond
of cyanide, catch the eye of the fruit seller
who thinks to slice the equator of an apple.

In the narrow street where kisses duplicate stars,
they find no layers to pull away, no surfaces,
yet rest on a marvellous tabletop nevertheless.

Dream Location

I take you to the riverbank where floats to a stop
the white blossom and the wings of insects

and in the secret places, the honey of the moon-rose
of the South, radiant white almost translucent

honey of merchandise, snowberry honey
of the sting of the bee, which drives us mad.

Nor can I be sure where the day went, whether
it had been hidden or unveiled so much so

I hadn't seen it. The swarm reaches its pitch.
Drowsing in the alphabet of a missing letter

I navigate in the meantime through storms,
all the while looking for the bee-black singularity

of their eyes that lead us back to that darkness
in which we see ourselves inside each other.

Desperate Meetings of Hermaphrodites

In the hotel on the other side of the mirror
the chaise longue dictates the poem of the film
can only be a snapshot, seeing as the film

is a book – and as it snaps shut it opens
again on a random page at any moment
of a keyhole or doorframe through which

you look for an unabridged view of whoever
has left their black brogue and white stiletto
in the corridor exchanged for a halo of the five

points of a star becoming the snap of a finger until
you're falling back through the smashed mirror
into the room – or so it looked – seeing as the mirror

is a poem, which, in any case, is made of water –
finding the dripping statue, from whose mouth
all this had come, is dressing up as you.

Notes

Re-reading Akhmatova: Akhmatova, known in her circle as the Russian Sappho, was unhappy with Robert Lowell's imitation of 'Requiem', published in 1961 before publication in Russia of her original.

Other Roads: *IV. Dun Holm*: Durham.

To St Mary Redcliffe: The epigraph and the 'acrostic' are from Thomas Norton's *The Ordinall of Alchimy*, the English version of which was not published until 1652 when it appeared in Ashmole's *Theatrum Chemicum Britannicum*. The story has it that Norton succeeded in making the Elixir of Life only for it to be stolen by the wife of William Canynges, who sold it and used the profits to rebuild the church of St Mary Redcliffe.

I have drawn material from E. J. Holmyard's *Alchemy,* and from Norton's manuscript in the Bristol Central Reference Library.

V. Coleridge married Sara Fricker in the church on 4th October 1795.

The Withdrawing Room: Set in the Georgian House Museum which once belonged to the sugar merchant, John Pinney, a member of the anti-abolitionist Bristol West India Society. Contrary to popular myth, it is highly unlikely that this is where Coleridge and Wordsworth first met, given that Coleridge was renowned at the time for his lectures calling for the abolition of slavery, delivered in Bristol city centre.

Rosary: The title of Akhmatova's second collection.

Fontannyy Dom: Fountain House, where the poet lived with her lover, Punin, his wife and daughter.

Bolshoy Fontan: Akhmatova's birthplace.

Annunciation in an Elevator: See Cocteau's poem 'L'Ange Heurtebise'.

The Charity of Thomas Rowley: See *The Collected Works of Thomas Chatterton, Volume I*, A Bicentenary Edition (London: Oxford University Press, 1971), p. 646.

Milestones: Epigraph from Coleridge's *Notebooks*. After a week of walking in burnt shoes, he finally bought a new pair in Fort Augustus. See *Breaking Away: Coleridge in Scotland*, Carol Kyros Walker (New Haven: Yale University Press, 2002), p. 180.

Tearing and Mending: Emmanuelle Riva also starred in Cocteau's *Thomas L'imposteur*.

Redressing Marsyas:

"Is he not like a Silenus in this? To be sure he is: his outer mask is the carved head of the Silenus; but O my companions

in drink, when he is opened, what temperance there is
residing within!" – Plato, *Symposium*

I have drawn from Edith Wyss' *The Myth of Apollo and
Marsyas in the Art of the Italian Renaissance* (London:
Associated University Presses, 1996).

The Garden Path: Epigraph adapted from Sappho's
Fragment 50, in Anne Carson's *If Not, Winter* (New York:
Vintage Books, 2002).

'True emblem' – this phrasing is borrowed from Don
Paterson's version of a Rilke sonnet, 'The Double Realm'
in *Orpheus* (London: Faber, 2006).

Dream Location: Song of Songs, 2:14.

Desperate Meetings of Hermaphrodites: See Cocteau's
film *Le Sang d'un Poète*.

General note: Repeated references to the name 'Thomas',
seven in total, were not intentional on behalf of the author
but can nevertheless be taken as referring to Didymus,
'The Twin'. In Aramaic 'Thomas' also means 'twin'.

Acknowledgements

Many thanks to the editors of the following magazines and publications in which some of these poems, or versions of them, first appeared:

The Echoing Gallery (Redcliffe Press), The Edinburgh Review, Granta, The Moth, New Statesman, Poetry London, The Scottish Poetry Library: Best Scottish Poems 2007, The Yellow Nib.

Versions of 'Balmerino Abbey' and 'Caritas' were first published in a limited edition anthology of poems by M.Litt. students, 2005–2006, *Stolen Weather* (Castle House Press, University of St Andrews). An early version of 'To St Mary Redcliffe' appeared in *Addicted to Brightness* (Long Lunch Press, 2006).

My thanks also to the Society of Authors for financial assistance; to A.H.B., Douglas Dunn and Don Paterson for their support and kindness. Special thanks are due to the Royal Literary Fund.